ALIENS

BY JOHN HAMILTON

VISIT US AT
WWW.ABDOPUBLISHING.COM

Published by ABDO Publishing Company, 4940 Viking Drive, Suite 622, Edina, Minnesota 55435.
Copyright ©2007 by Abdo Consulting Group, Inc. International copyrights reserved in all countries.
No part of this book may be reproduced in any form without written permission from the publisher.
ABDO & Daughters™ is a trademark and logo of ABDO Publishing Company.

Printed in the United States.

Editor: Sue Hamilton
Graphic Design: John Hamilton
Cover Design: Neil Klinepier
Cover Illustration: Photo Researchers
Interior Photos and Illustrations: p 1 green alien, Photo Researchers; p 4 cat-eyed alien, Corbis;
p 5 UFOs hover over city, Corbis; p 6 *Close Encounters*, courtesy Columbia Pictures; p 7 *The Day the
Earth Stood Still*, courtesy Twentieth Century Fox; p 8 illustration from *The War of the Worlds*, Mary
Evans; p 9 illustration from cover of *Amazing Stories*, Corbis; p 10 (top) scene from *The War of the Worlds*,
courtesy Paramount Pictures; (bottom) scene from *War of the Worlds*, courtesy Paramount Pictures/
DreamWorks SKG; p 11 H.G. Wells, Getty Images; p 12 *Mars Attacks!*, AP Images; p 13 Aliens land,
Corbis; p 14 *Starship Troopers*, Corbis; p 15 *Invasion of the Body Snatchers*, courtesy Republic Pictures;
X-Files, courtesy 20th Century Fox; p 17 creature from *Alien*, AP Images; p 18 (top) *Space Invaders*,
courtesy Bally, (bottom) *DOOM 3*, courtesy id Software; p 19 (top) *StarCraft*, courtesy Blizzard
Entertainment, (bottom) *Gears of War*, courtesy Epic Games; p 20 (top) Mexican UFOs, AP Images,
(bottom) crop circle, AP Images; p 21 three aliens landing, Photo Researchers; p 22 alien abductee holds
x-ray, Corbis; p 23 cows abducted by flying saucer, iStockphoto; p 24 Roswell debris, Photo Researchers;
p 25 Roswell crash, Photo Researchers; p 26 alien fetus, Photo Researchers; p 27 view of Area 51, courtesy
SpaceImaging.com; p 28 Parkes radio telescope, Photo Researchers; p 29 alien with colored eyes, Corbis.

Library of Congress Cataloging-in-Publication Data

Hamilton, John, 1959-
 Aliens / John Hamilton.
     p. cm. -- (The world of horror)
 Includes index.
 ISBN-13: 978-1-59928-766-9
 ISBN-10: 1-59928-766-8
 1. Human-alien encounters. 2. Unidentified flying objects--Sightings and encounters. 3. Curiosities and
wonders. I. Title.
 BF2050.H36 2007
 001.942--dc22
                              2006032726

CONTENTS

LOOK TO THE SKIES!

Within the world of horror lurk all kinds of beasties: vampires, werewolves, sea monsters, ghosts. There is a seemingly endless list of things that we love to be scared of. Just before the turn of the 20th century, other creatures emerged that grabbed hold of our fears. Aliens, those strange, otherworldly, sometimes bug-eyed menaces from outer space, have been haunting our dreams for more than 100 years. Today, they're as popular as ever. In literature, television, and movies, aliens continue to fascinate and terrify us.

When aliens come to Earth, it can be humbling and wondrous. Who doesn't love E.T., the cuddly alien from Steven Spielberg's *E.T. the Extraterrestrial*? But more often, alien encounters are horrifying. The invading Martians of H.G. Wells' *The War of the Worlds* nearly wipe out humanity in just a few days. Sometimes we don't even know when aliens live among us.

Facing page: A pair of disk-shaped UFOs hovers over a nighttime cityscape.
Below: A green-skinned alien with cat-like eyes.

In *Men in Black*, government agents keep track of aliens in disguise, who are hidden from a blissfully ignorant public.

What are aliens? Usually, we think of them as intelligent, sentient creatures. Some are good, some are bad. Others just want a good meal. Aliens are almost always from a distant planet, although sometimes they live practically next door, on Mars, or even as close as Earth's moon.

Aliens come in all shapes and sizes. Some are humanoid, resembling ordinary Earthlings. Others are insectoids, like talking cockroaches with big brains. Some are scaly reptilians, while some have no shape at all, like gaseous blobs floating on the breeze.

CLOSE ENCOUNTERS

People have certain ideas about aliens. If beings from other planets are ugly and have sharp teeth, they must certainly be hostile to people. This is a common way of viewing anyone from outside our own culture. If the outsiders don't meet our standards of beauty, or they dress differently than us, we're automatically suspicious. But maybe aliens are more like us than we think. Maybe they're just trying to get a job done so they can go home.

Many stories about aliens start out dark and suspenseful. We're led to believe that the extraterrestrials have evil intentions. But then we discover a much different truth. In the 1953 movie classic *It Came From Outer Space*, invading aliens turn out to be nothing more than stranded intergalactic travelers who are just trying to repair their spaceship so they can leave Earth. It's a similar theme to 1982's *E.T. the Extra-Terrestrial*, in which E.T., the alien main character, only wants to "go home."

Below: The alien mother ship from Steven Spielberg's *Close Encounters of the Third Kind*.

In director Steven Spielberg's 1977 science-fiction classic *Close Encounters of the Third Kind*, spindly armed aliens travel to Earth in a huge "mother ship." The aliens begin abducting people, seemingly at random. Government scientists finally figure out how to communicate with the extraterrestrials using musical notes. The aliens want to take specially selected humans into space on their ship, for reasons that are never revealed. This sounds scary at first. But for the people who are chosen, the trip promises to be wondrous and enlightening. The title of the film refers to the final stage of an alien sighting: actual contact with extraterrestrial beings.

In *The Day the Earth Stood Still*, the 1951 classic science-fiction film by Robert Wise, humanity fails a crucial test. A superior alien named Klaatu lands in a flying saucer in Washington, D.C. After observing humans and noting their violent ways, he finally makes an announcement to the startled Earthlings. Klaatu warns the world that his alien race will not tolerate the humans' development and use of nuclear weapons. Klaatu says that his people do not particularly care if humans destroy themselves, but if mankind becomes too warlike and ventures into space, threatening the intergalactic neighborhood, then Klaatu's alien forces promise to blow up Earth. As a demonstration of the aliens' power, Klaatu is accompanied by a large, silver-clad robot named Gort, who can melt a tank with a single glance from his heat-ray visor.

Above: The alien robot Gort stands guard next to his flying saucer in this scene from *The Day the Earth Stood Still.*

THE WAR OF THE WORLDS

The root of all alien invasion stories can be found in H.G. Wells' *The War of the Worlds.* More than 100 years after its publication in 1898, the story continues to frighten and fascinate us. As we cast a suspicious eye toward the stars, we wonder: are there really aliens up there, watching us, plotting our destruction?

Herbert George Wells (1866-1946) was an important English writer famous for his science-fiction novels. He wrote more than 80 books, including *The Time Machine* in 1895, and *The Invisible Man* in 1897. Science-fiction author and teacher James Gunn called Wells, "the man who invented tomorrow."

Wells was born on September 21, 1866, in Bromley, Kent, southeast of London, England. He grew up in near-poverty. His father was a failed shopkeeper, and his mother was a maid. When he was seven years old, Wells suffered a badly broken leg, which required him to stay indoors for many weeks in order to heal. To pass the time, his mother brought him books to read. Wells fell in love with the great works of fiction. He was determined to become a writer himself one day. Wells later wrote that his broken leg was "one of the luckiest events of my life."

Facing page: An illustration by Blade Gallentine, which was used on the cover of the August 1929 issue of *Amazing Stories. Right:* A Martian exits his spaceship, from a 1906 edition of *The War of the Worlds.*

Above: A Martian fighting machine from the 1953 film version of *The War of the Worlds.*

Many people consider *The War of the Worlds* to be Wells' best novel. In the story, aliens from Mars flee their dying planet, landing on Earth in giant cylinder-shaped rockets. They begin their invasion by attacking London. The Martians use huge "fighting machines," which are pods on top of three long, metal legs. The aliens' weapons include "heat rays" and toxic black smoke. Humans are helpless against the technologically superior Martians. Victory seems certain for the invaders, but within days they mysteriously begin dropping dead. In one of the great plot twists of science fiction, the Martians become infected by Earth germs, of which the aliens have no natural defense. Humanity is saved by the smallest of creatures.

The War of the Worlds was so successful that many remakes and imitations were made over the years. On Halloween eve, October 30, 1938, actor Orson Welles and the Mercury Theatre produced a radio broadcast version of the story. It featured fake news reports, amazing sound effects, and on-the-spot reporting. Some people believed the invasion was really happening. They panicked, rushing into the streets and fleeing the cities to escape the "alien invasion."

In 1953, Hollywood producer George Pal created a movie version of Wells' novel. These modern, updated Martians flew in green manta ray-shaped craft. The machines had probes in front, like a cobra's head, which spewed death rays. The dizzying visual and sound effects made *The War of the Worlds* a movie classic. It won the 1953 Academy Award for best special effects.

In 2005, director Steven Spielberg brought yet another version of *The War of the Worlds* to movie theaters. This time actor Tom Cruise plays a man who flees New York City with his children as alien invaders begin a reign of destruction. Spielberg used several elements from Wells' original novel, including giant tripod-legged fighting machines and death rays, while updating the story for modern audiences.

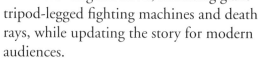

Left: From left to right, actors Tim Robbins, Tom Cruise, and Dakota Fanning cower from invading Martians in this scene from Steven Spielberg's *War of the Worlds.*

Above: H.G. Wells, author of *The War of the Worlds.*

ALIEN INVASION!

Facing page: A group of invading space aliens. *Below:* A hideous alien from Tim Burton's *Mars Attacks!*

Following the success of *The War of the Worlds*, many science-fiction and horror novels and movies have imitated the alien invasion formula. For example, in 1996, Roland Emmerich and Dean Devlin created *Independence Day*, a blockbuster movie featuring giant spacecraft, hostile aliens, and death rays. In Tim Burton's 1996 film *Mars Attacks!*, the earth is invaded by flying saucers filled with hostile, big-headed Martians, who use ray guns to kill humans because it's fun.

There are many reasons why aliens would invade Earth. They might want our oxygen or our water. Perhaps they're warlike beings that are making their way across the galaxy, and Earth is simply next on their list. Of course, sometimes aliens are just trying to survive. Maybe they think humans are a tasty source of food.

In the story *To Serve Man*, author Damon Knight wrote about a race of aliens who land on Earth. At first, the aliens are nice to humans. They stop all wars, hunger, and poverty. The reason they are so helpful, the aliens explain, is because of a mysterious book, which hadn't been translated into any human language. The only thing the humans know is that the book's title is *To Serve Man*. Humans are soon invited to the aliens' home planet, and they eagerly line up like lambs to a slaughter. Only at the end of the story does the hero discover—too late—that the mysterious book is, in fact, a cookbook. Humans are being sent to the alien planet as the main course in an extraterrestrial feast.

Other aliens, instead of tricking people, use brute force to destroy humanity. Rather than little green men, these aliens are weird and terrifying. They are such a cliché in science fiction and horror stories that they've been given a nickname: BEM, which stands for "bug-eyed monster." From the shape-changing creature in 1951's *The Thing From Another World,* to the giant, hostile, alien bugs of Robert Heinlein's *Starship Troopers*, audiences have screamed in delight whenever BEMs show their ugly faces.

In the 1950s and early 1960s, people were afraid that the spread of nuclear weapons would destroy the world, or the spewed radiation would cause horrifying mutations. A rash of

giant, radiation-caused monsters invaded movie theaters all over the world. Godzilla, Rodan, and countless giant insects were all spawned in a haze of radioactive fear.

Fear also brought about alien invasion movies in which the creatures are hidden among us, often taking control of our minds and bodies. Many of these stories were popular because of the Cold War, the conflict in the mid-20th century between the democracies of the West, led by the United States, and Communist dictatorships led by China and the Soviet Union. People feared that secret Communist agents might take over the U.S. government. It was hard to tell who was a friend and who was an enemy. This fear was reflected in our popular culture, especially in movies. The most famous example is the 1956 film *Invasion of the Body Snatchers*, in which a doctor discovers that his town's residents are being replaced by alien duplicates. The movie's producers said it was never intended to be a response to the Cold War, but for many people it reflected perfectly the paranoia that gripped the nation during that time.

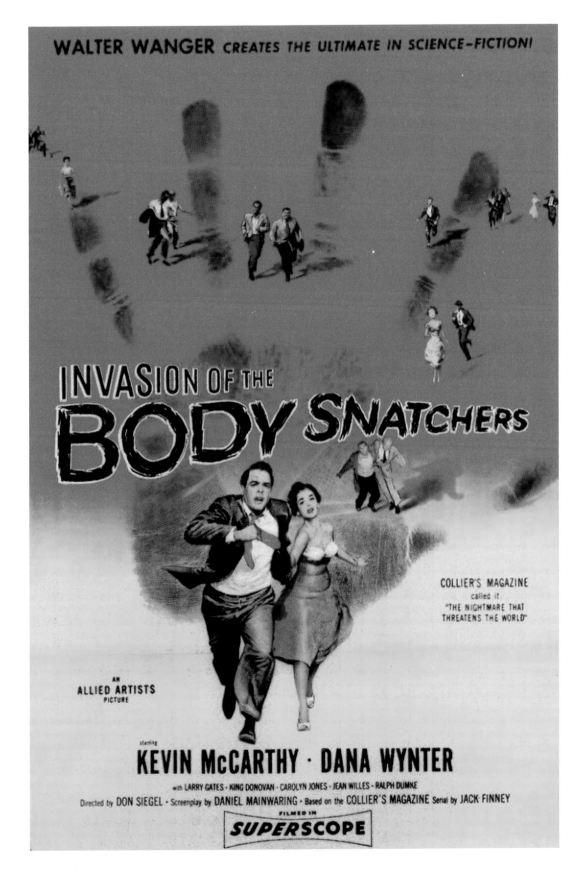

WALTER WANGER CREATES THE ULTIMATE IN SCIENCE-FICTION!

INVASION OF THE BODY SNATCHERS

COLLIER'S MAGAZINE called it "THE NIGHTMARE THAT THREATENS THE WORLD"

AN ALLIED ARTISTS PICTURE

starring

KEVIN McCARTHY · DANA WYNTER

with LARRY GATES · KING DONOVAN · CAROLYN JONES · JEAN WILLES · RALPH DUMKE

Directed by DON SIEGEL · Screenplay by DANIEL MAINWARING · Based on the COLLIER'S MAGAZINE Serial by JACK FINNEY

FILMED IN SUPERSCOPE

Unidentified Flying Objects (UFOs), rampaging aliens, pod people, and giant radioactive bugs all reflect our fear of invasion and destruction. But sometimes aliens aren't so easy to spot. They're often cloaked behind secrecy and government conspiracy. *The X-Files* played on that fear very successfully during its nine seasons on television. FBI agents Fox Mulder and Dana Scully continually uncovered shady plots of alien domination. They fought not only the invaders, but also people in the United States government who wanted to keep things secret.

Sometimes aliens can be microscopic, as in Michael Crichton's 1969 thriller *The Andromeda Strain*, which was also made into a movie in 1971. The story involves scientists who desperately try to isolate and destroy a deadly virus that has hitchhiked back to Earth aboard a space probe. It's a cautionary tale about military blundering, and how Earth's gravest threat may come not from spaceships and death rays, but from the smallest of organisms, a sort of *The War of the Worlds* in reverse.

The Cold War, plus our suspicions of government and new technology, are often used to explain stories of alien conquest. Sometimes, though, a scary alien is simply a substitute for a ghost story. Ridley Scott's 1979 film *Alien* is often described as a haunted house story set in outer space. The creatures in *Alien*, as well as its sequels, are some of the most imaginative and horrifying ever created.

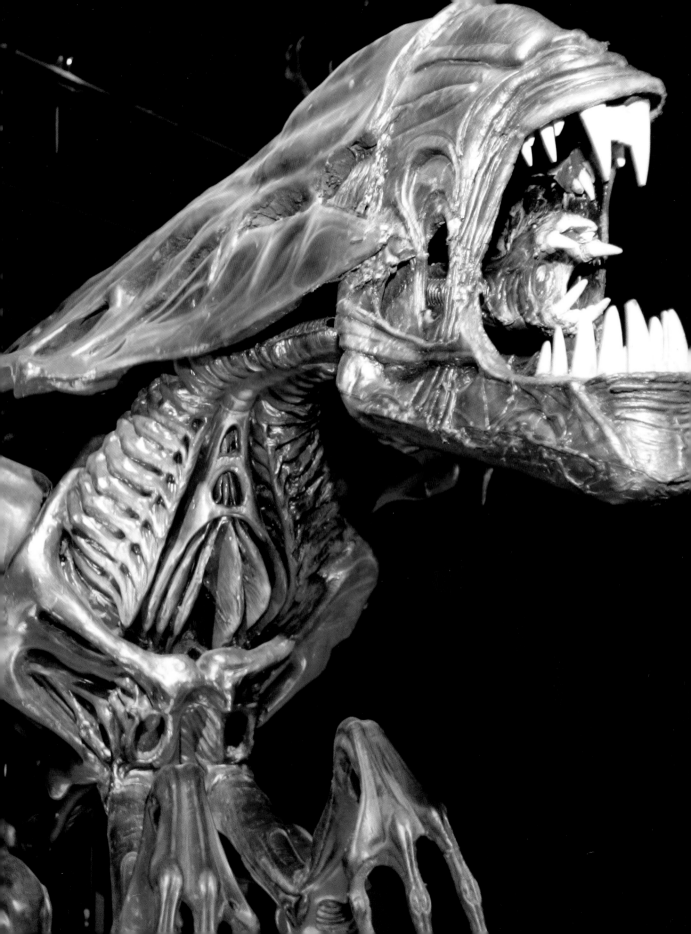

ALIENS IN VIDEO GAMES

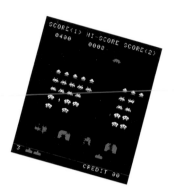

More and more people today turn to computers and video games for their entertainment. Storytellers have taken advantage of recent advances in technology to create original, riveting tales of alien invasions, not to mention hours of gaming fun!

The granddaddy of alien video games is *Space Invaders*. First released in Japan in 1978, the game quickly became a smash hit worldwide, and influenced countless future video games. Although the computer graphics are primitive by today's standards, *Space Invaders* had an addictive quality that kept players plunking down their quarters for just one more try.

In 1993, id Software released *DOOM*, an innovative 3-D game for personal computers in which players become space marines battling Earth-invading aliens. The aliens of *DOOM* are

Above right: Space Invaders, the classic alien-invasion game of the late 1970s. *Below:* A screenshot from *DOOM 3.*

grotesque and vicious, ranging from imps and spiders to red, floating cacodemons. *DOOM* was one of the most popular video games of all time, spawning several sequels and a 2005 movie starring Dwayne "The Rock" Johnson. In 2004, id Software updated the game by releasing *DOOM 3*, with advanced graphics and terrifying sound effects.

StarCraft, and its sequel, *StarCraft: Brood War*, are strategy games in which players fight for the survival of humankind. *StarCraft* was released in 1998. Both games are produced by Blizzard Entertainment. Players can choose to be Terrans (humans), or one of two alien races: the mighty, technologically advanced Protoss, or the swarming, insect-like Zerg.

Modern video games take advantage of the most powerful graphics and sound effects available for the home, including computer platforms and gaming consoles such as the Xbox 360 and PlayStation 3. This combination of advanced technology creates a very realistic gaming experience, which can be terrifying when battling invading space aliens. Some of the most exciting alien villains of recent video games include the Aliens from *Halo*, the head-crabs from *Half-Life*, and the Locust from *Gears of War*.

Above: Humans battle the insect-like Zerg in this screenshot from Blizzard's *StarCraft: Brood War.*
Below: A screenshot from the thrilling video game *Gears of War*, in which humans battle creatures called the Locust Horde.

UFOs

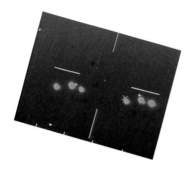

Above right: An image taken by Mexican air force pilots on March 5, 2004. This series of brightly lit, rapidly moving objects was filmed in the skies over Mexico. The lights may have been gases in the atmosphere, but the exact cause remains unsolved.
Facing page: An artist's rendering of a UFO landing.
Below: Crop circles found in a Montour, Iowa, soybean field on September 3, 2002.

Aliens come to Earth in various ways. By far the most common method of transportation is the ever-popular flying saucer. When humans encounter a strange craft in the sky that they cannot identify, it is called an unidentified flying object, or UFO.

Sightings of what we think of as flying saucers became more common shortly after World War II. On June 24, 1947, the first modern UFO was spotted by a man flying a private plane over Washington's Mount Rainier. The pilot reported that he saw nine bright, saucer-shaped objects flying at high speed near the mountain. Since then, tens of thousands of people have reported seeing UFOs. Most of these sightings are later explained as strange weather phenomena, experimental aircraft, or even weather balloons. But many sightings remain a mystery. Could there really be aliens secretly visiting our planet?

Most UFOs are shaped like flying disks. Others are cigar shaped. Some have bright lights and spin like a top, while others hover noiselessly in midair. Almost all UFOs fly through the atmosphere at high speed. The U.S. Air Force began investigating UFO reports in the late 1940s in what was eventually called Project Blue Book. By the late 1960s, the Air Force stopped its investigation. It concluded that nearly all UFOs were either natural phenomena, like clouds and swamp gas, or were hoaxes.

Many people are still convinced that aliens are visiting Earth. They point to the existence of crop circles as proof. Crop circles

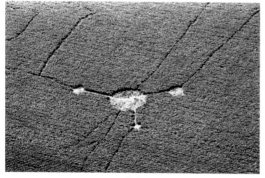

are the geometric patterns of flattened crops, as if a heavy spacecraft has landed in a field. Most crop circles have been found in England, but they have also appeared in other parts of the world. Some people have confessed to creating the mysterious circles in the middle of the night using boards to flatten the crops. Still, many crop circles remain unexplained.

ALIEN ABDUCTION

Many people insist that aliens and UFOs are real. Why are they so sure? Because, they claim, they've been abducted by aliens. Most alien kidnappings have eerie similarities. A person is first taken from a room, or transported by an energy beam, into an alien ship, sometimes a flying saucer. Once inside the ship, the abductees are medically examined by aliens. These extraterrestrial creatures are often described as short, gray-skinned beings with huge, saucer-like eyes. After the exam, the aliens may give tours of their ship, or take the victims on rides through space. When abductees are finally returned home, they often lose track of time, as if they've lost a part of their memory. Afterwards, many abductees report feelings of sickness and shame. Many are afraid to come forward with their stories for fear of being ridiculed.

Below: UFO abductee Bruce May shows an x-ray of his shoulder, which he claims was operated on by aliens when he was abducted near Rachel, Nevada.

One of the most famous cases of alien abduction occurred in 1961. Betty and Barney Hill lived in Portsmouth, New Hampshire. While driving home one night on an isolated country road, they reportedly saw a bright point of light in the sky, which they soon discovered was a disk-shaped UFO, with aliens inside. The couple raced home, but began have recurring nightmares soon afterwards. In their dreams, they each recalled entering the UFO, where they claim they

were examined by large-eyed aliens, and then returned back to Earth. Psychologists think the couple might have suffered from a shared hallucination, or perhaps some other kind of mental illness. The Hills, however, steadfastly insisted that they were the victims of alien abduction.

Humans aren't the only creatures who are the objects of extraterrestrial kidnappings. Sometimes livestock is found mutilated under mysterious circumstances. The victims are usually cows, although sheep and horses have also been mutilated. Natural causes, such as predators and scavengers, may have caused the grisly killings, but some people are convinced that aliens are responsible. They theorize that the aliens are experimenting on the livestock to learn about Earth creatures.

Above: Many people believe that mutilated cattle discovered on farms and ranches around the country have been experimented on by aliens.

THE ROSWELL CRASH

Below: An Army officer kneels next to debris collected at the Roswell UFO crash site. The U.S. government declared that the wreckage was part of a weather balloon.

In June 1947, farmer William Brazel discovered strange wreckage on his ranch near the town of Roswell, New Mexico. He and his family gathered up the materials, which consisted of shards of rubber and large sheets of some kind of metallic material, like tinfoil. After reporting his find to the local sheriff, several plainclothes men visited the ranch. They said they were from the nearby Roswell Army Air Field. After collecting additional debris from the ranch, they took the material back to their base.

The Army concluded that the debris was the wreckage of a top-secret weather balloon, along with a silver-clad radar reflector. In July, the local newspaper, the *Roswell Daily Record*, printed a story that claimed the Army had recovered the wreckage of a flying saucer. This caused a stir, but the official military response gave the same story: the material from Brazel's ranch was a weather balloon.

Year later, some witnesses came forward who claimed the Army actually recovered the wreckage of a

UFO, and then hid the evidence. The Army covered up the truth, these people say, so that the advanced alien spaceship technology could be secretly studied. These witnesses even claimed that the dead bodies of several aliens were taken back to the Roswell base, where autopsies were performed to learn more about the mysterious extraterrestrials.

Most people think that the Roswell incident really was just a weather balloon, and that people who claim otherwise are continuing a big hoax. But there are some elements of the alien cover-up and conspiracy theory that have never been adequately explained. To this day, many people still believe that humans actually made contact with alien beings out in the New Mexico desert in 1947.

Above: A painting of the Roswell UFO incident. Some people believe an alien spacecraft was struck by lightning before it crashed near Roswell, New Mexico, in 1947.

AREA 51

rea 51, also known as Groom Lake, is a U.S. Air Force base deep in the Nevada desert, about 90 miles (145 km) north of Las Vegas. It is a top-secret facility that is used to test experimental aircraft before they are revealed to the public. The U-2 spy plane and F-117 Nighthawk "stealth" fighter were both tested at Area 51.

The government land surrounding Area 51 is strictly off-limits to the public. Curiosity seekers who approach the base are turned away by armed guards. Underground motion sensors and helicopter surveillance give added security.

Below: Could the government be hiding the bodies of dead aliens at Area 51?

Partly because of the secrecy surrounding Area 51, many people believe the U.S. government examines and tests captured alien UFOs at the base. There are many unusual phenomena that happen around Area 51, including strange lights flying around the surrounding countryside at night. In 1989, a man claimed in an interview with a Las Vegas television station that he once worked on an alien spacecraft near the facility.

Some people believe that the U.S. government has captured a UFO and is studying it in a laboratory hidden deep underground. Government scientists, these people claim, are trying to "reverse engineer" the spaceship's advanced technology for use in U.S. aircraft. Other theories about Area 51 activities include time travel, weather control, and research on alien energy weapons. One witness even claimed to have videotape of an alien being questioned by government interrogators.

TOP SECRET!
ALIEN FETUS
July 8, 1947
Air Field (RAAF)
RAAF 509th Bomb Group
DO NOT OPEN

Whether or not any of these theories are true, the United States government isn't saying. It will not discuss the top-secret base. Townships near Area 51, however, have taken advantage of the base's fame. Many tourists travel through the area, hoping for a glimpse of an alien craft drifting across the sky. In 1996, Nevada State Route 375, the 98-mile (158 km) road running north of Area 51, was renamed "The Extraterrestrial Highway."

Above: Area 51 can be seen in this satellite image. The top-secret base is about 90 miles (145 km) north of Las Vegas, Nevada.

REAL ALIENS?

Are there really aliens roaming through outer space? Will they someday visit Earth? Or have they already visited our planet? There's no evidence that proves the existence of alien life. But astronomers believe there's a good chance life exists in other solar systems. The universe holds trillions of stars. Many undoubtedly have the right conditions for life, which most scientists say include liquid water and temperatures similar to Earth's. Alien life may resemble simple bacteria, or it may be an advanced civilization capable of space travel. It might even be something so bizarre that we don't recognize it as a life form.

If life does exist on other planets, why haven't they made themselves known to us? Some believe that aliens have already made contact. As proof, they point to the many UFO sightings made over the last century. They believe governments and the military hide the existence of alien visitors in order to prevent people from panicking.

A more likely reason, however, is that aliens haven't discovered our little out-of-the-way planet just yet. Most people don't realize just how big our universe really is. Our galaxy alone, the Milky Way, is so immense that it takes light 100,000 years just to cross from one end to the other. It contains more than 100 billion stars. And the distance between the stars is incredibly vast. Finding Earth would be harder than finding a needle in a haystack.

Left: The Parkes radio telescope in New South Wales, Australia, is often used by the SETI (Search for Extra-Terrestrial Intelligence) Institute. The rotating dish has a diameter of 210 feet (64 m).

Some believe the most practical way to make alien contact is by monitoring radio waves. The SETI Institute began in the 1960s with the goal of searching for intelligent life in other parts of our galaxy. SETI stands for "Search for Extra-Terrestrial Intelligence." The SETI Institute scans deep space with huge telescopes that detect radio waves, searching for possible alien signals. It's not an easy task. Space is huge, and there are many radio frequencies to search. After years of listening, with help from the most advanced computers available, nothing yet has been detected. But the hunt continues. If an alien signal finally reaches Earth, it will answer a question that has haunted mankind for thousands of years: are we alone? Is anybody else out there?

Above: Most astronomers believe there is a good chance that alien life exists in other solar systems.

GLOSSARY

BEM

A word sometimes used in science-fiction stories, which stands for "bug-eyed monster."

COLD WAR

The mainly diplomatic conflict waged between the United States and the former Soviet Union after World War II. The Cold War resulted in a large buildup of weapons and troops. It ended when the Soviet Union broke up in the late 1980s and early 1990s.

EARTHLING

An inhabitant of the planet Earth. In science fiction, an alien might call a human being an Earthling.

EXTRATERRESTRIAL

Something that comes from outside the earth or its atmosphere. In most science-fiction stories, an extraterrestrial is a sentient alien from another planet.

GALAXY

A system of millions, or even hundreds of billions, of stars and planets, clustered together in a distinct shape, like a spiral or ellipse. Earth is located within the Milky Way Galaxy.

HUMANOID

Looking like or behaving like a human being. A humanoid alien would typically have a torso, four limbs, and a head.

PARANOIA

A fear, or suspicion, of people or their actions, even when there's no direct evidence of harm. In the mid-20th century, many Americans had a paranoia about Communist countries, such as the former Soviet Union and China. This fear showed up in the kinds of movies people liked to watch, especially science-fiction films about sneaky invading aliens. A good example is *Invasion of the Body Snatchers*.

SENTIENT

Able to have feelings, or sense feelings in others. It can also mean simply being conscious, with an awareness of the outside world. For example, in science fiction, a sentient alien would be able to communicate with humans from Earth, or at least be aware of their presence. A simple microbe, or germ, from another planet would not be sentient (unless it's a very special microbe beyond our current understanding of what defines "life" and "consciousness").

SETI INSTITUTE

A group that uses a system of large telescopes and receiver dishes to monitor radio waves in the search for extraterrestrial life. SETI stands for "Search for Extra-Terrestrial Intelligence."

UFO

An Unidentified Flying Object. In science fiction, a UFO is typically some kind of alien craft, such as a flying saucer.

Below: Several major characters in the popular science-fiction television series *Farscape* are aliens.

INDEX